THE INTERVIEWER'S
No Brainer
GUIDE TO GETTING HIRED

Basic tips and tricks to landing the job you want
(short, sweet, and to the point)

Leena Lavage

FORWARD

Feeling frustrated while trying to hire new employees in the dental office where I am Office Manager, I decided to write a book. That's how frustrated I was while looking for the right candidate. During a time when the job market is so-called sparse, I have gone through six weeks (so far) of interviews and working interviews, and I still haven't hired the right person. It's not that I'm being that picky! I'm looking for energy and common sense. This is a sort of "Hand Book" on what to do and what not to do during interviews in any field.

I've been in the dental business for over 25 years, on both ends, being the hirer and the person who was hired. Everything in this book is factual- meaning I have seen it, experienced it, or from good sources know this has happened to them. I honestly couldn't make up some of the experiences I have had.

It doesn't matter in which field you are interested in working, even though this book gives examples of doctor's offices. These strategies apply to medical offices, as well as insurance agencies, or anywhere else. It's basic. A lot is common sense, a lot is being "on the other end" and explaining to you what the hiring person sees. I am not sugar-coating anything, and at times I *may* seem blunt. I want to help you have a good interview and find the great job you deserve.

I hope you take this to heart and this enables you to find the perfect job. Best wishes.

CONTENTS

Your Resume
Your Phone and
Return Calls
Dressing For Your
Interview
Group Interview
Previous Employers
Personal Information
Working Interview
OMG I'm Gonna Be
Late!
Basic Common Sense
You Got The Job
The End

YOUR RESUME

There are a ton of websites that will guide you in creating the perfect resume. I am not going to spend time on that. However, I am going to guide you on what to put into it.

First of all, no fancy format. Chances are you are replying to an ad online, which means you will be emailing or attaching your resume to an email in response to an ad. I have seen too many resumes with an extreme set-up, but when I would print it, it lost all appeal. More importantly, it was hard to read. Stick to a traditional resume with an easy to read font. When you go to an interview, bring a hardcopy of your resume. It is appropriate to print it on an off-white stationary, or beige, as long as it looks business-like. This is not *Legally Blonde*, no colored stationary and DO NOT scent it.

Be sure your information is accurate. I'm not kidding. I received a resume that looked very promising. When I phoned her to schedule an interview, her phone number was disconnected. So I tried the second number on the resume. That was also disconnected. There was an email address, but I was not emailing people. I wanted to hear how they sounded on the phone and ask a few basic questions. So I tossed the resume. If she wasn't detailed enough to have working phone numbers (in her case, two) on the resume, how could I trust her with patient information?

Be sure your work history is in order, from present to the last seven years. The exceptions are if you've been in your industry for twenty years, be sure the dates are accurate. If you are fresh out of school, enter those dates. Do not leave any gaps. For example, if you worked for Dr. Jones from May of 2005 to July of 2011, then you worked for Dr. Smith from July of 2011 to January of 2013, and it is now July of 2014, what have you been doing since your last job? Gaps in work history are flags. Flags are not a good thing.

It is totally appropriate if you say, "I left Dr. Smith in January of 2013 to have a baby, and now I am ready and excited about getting back into the work force." If you say you left to take care of a sick parent, and you are now ready and excited to get back into the work force, that is good. Do not leave it blank and think to yourself that you will explain what you have been doing the last 16 months at an interview. You may not get the interview because of this. Also, do not think it will look bad if you left the industry for awhile and took a break or tried something new. This is not uncommon. It shows you were working, had the courage to try something new, and are not limiting yourself. Put something down.

YOUR PHONE AND RETURN CALLS

When a potential employer calls a candidate, they listen. What is the message on your phone? If I call someone and the message is, "Yeah hey it's me, Ash, you know the drill," I immediately think I have someone immature. If you have a cutesy message, change it until you find a job! This reflects you! Don't think to yourself, "Well that's me, I'm friendly and light-hearted." That's fine, but your employer hears it as, "She's not serious and she's immature." A proper message doesn't have to be stuffy, just simple. "This is Ashley, I'm sorry I missed your call, please leave a message and I will get back to you, thank you." After you start your new job change your message back to anything you want.

If an employer does leave a message and asks you to call back, what you say when you call back is equally important.

"This is Ashley, you called me?" I really received this call, actually several times. Remember, you are calling back a *doctor's office*. You are not the only person that calls that day! Listen carefully to the message you received. I guarantee the caller left her name and most likely the doctor's name or practice name. Since you are calling her back, be prepared.

Call the office back and say, "Hi, this is Ashley Jones, Carol called me earlier and left a message regarding my resume, is she available?" This gives the person who answers your call all the information she needs. You're also making a good first impression. Even though Carol may be the one hiring, if Nancy answered the phone and received the call like I did (this is Ashley you called me?) she will tell Carol about it and how she scrambled trying to figure out if Ashley was a patient and what the call was about.

Have a list of questions, all which are important to YOU, regarding the job. Narrow this down to questions which will immediately tell you if you are interested in this office and want to secure an interview. For example, if you are looking for full-time job, ask if this position is full-time and about how many hours. Some offices consider full time 32 hours a week. You may want 40 hours a week. If they say its three days and you want five, ask if five days is a possibility. If the days are firm and not what you are looking for, pass on the interview. If the time of day is important to you, in other words, if you need to be home when your kids get home from school, ask what the hours are. If you are flexible and it really doesn't matter, don't waste that question for the phone call. Do ask about basic responsibilities. Don't go into questions about vacation time or sick pay, that's for the interview. You can ask the pay range. Range is important here. Most offices pay on experience. You know what you're worth and what you want. If you are looking for $15 an hour and they say the range is $14-16, that's good. If you want $20 an hour, and they say the range is $15-18, ask if the salary is negotiable. It is completely appropriate for you to say you are looking for a higher pay. Don't waste your time or theirs.

Be realistic. If you are moving from Los Angeles or New York City, where salaries (and everything else) are higher, and you are moving to a more reasonably priced part of the country, don't think you will get what you were making, no matter how good you are. It will not happen. Just like your cost of living will drop, so will your salary.

I interviewed a very qualified person who just moved from Los Angeles to Phoenix. When salary came up, she just kept quoting me what she was getting at a temp agency in California. She wanted the same salary. I nicely tried to explain to her that she was out of range, and did the house price comparison. Didn't matter, she wanted California salary. I wished her well and shredded her resume.

DRESSING FOR YOUR INTERVIEW

Oh boy. You would think this chapter would be easy. I'm going to start by telling you what NOT to wear:

Do not get dressed up as if you are going to a club.
Do not wear flip flops.
Do not wear jeans.
Do not wear obviously worn sweaters or things with holes in them.
Do not wear extremely short skirts, ones in which you have a hard time sitting.
Do not wear low tops with your cleavage showing.
Do not wear tank tops.
Do not wear a ton of perfume.
Do not carry a purse large enough to fit an animal.
Do not wear extremely high heels.
Do not come with your hair uncombed.
Do not wear a ton of make-up.
Do not wear T-shirts (guys or girls).
Do not wear golf shirts.
Do not wear any kind of tennis shoes (unless you are wearing scrubs).

I have interviewed people dressed with all of the above. They were not hired.

Wear business appropriate attire. If you have a suit, wear it. If it is a basic color you can add a little color: gray suit, red top underneath (this is also the only time a tank top is appropriate). If you don't own a suit, or it's outdated, wear dress pants or a skirt with an appropriate top. This would be a nice sweater, pretty top, or scrubs! It's a doctor's office! If you have a pair of scrubs and nothing else seems appropriate, wear them. (Side note on this: if you are applying for an office manager position, they might want you to wear business clothes, so for that position I would not wear scrubs to an interview). Guys, you do not need to wear a full suit unless you are applying for an office manager position with a group of doctors. If you are applying for a hygienist position, dental assistant, medical assistant, or x-ray tech, wear dress pants and a button-down shirt. Tie is optional. Be clean shaven and don't go heavy on the after-shave. Please comb your hair. If you wear it in a pony tail, that's fine. Make it neat. Nice shoes! Scrubs apply to you also.

Examples of people appropriately dressed: one woman came in wearing a white button-down, short-sleeve shirt, gray skirt, red belt, red shoes, hair pulled back in a ponytail. She looked great and was called back. A woman came in wearing black dress pants, a white button-down top, dressy high-heeled sandals, hair down but very pretty, average make-up. She was asked back for a working interview. One young girl, 20 years old, fresh out of school, walked in wearing a black suit with a white top underneath, nice shoes, and looked very much the business part. Not only was she asked back, she was hired. A guy wearing gray dress pants, button-down shirt (that matched), dress shoes that had a shine, clean shaven around his goatee. He was asked back.

Even if you live in an area which basically is "laid back," dress up for the interview. You will impress.

Remember the rule which applies to *everything*- it is better to be overdressed than underdressed.

GROUP INTERVIEW

Group interviews are very interesting. Honestly, when my boss told me we were going to have one, I wasn't too thrilled. But we did, and it ended up being very educational. For me.

The purpose of a group interview is to cut to the chase. In our instance, we had been interviewing for weeks, and the individual interviews were taking a toll. A group interview is more beneficial for the employer, but I will tell you how to succeed. Most places that have group interviews will let the candidate know this before hand. You need to follow protocol, but here are some tips on how to stand out.

Don't be on time, be early. If you don't know where the office is, for heaven's sake google the address, or better yet, drive by beforehand. Do all of the prior recommended things, dress appropriately, (inappropriate dress will immediately stick out in a crowd of appropriately dressed candidates). Bring your resume. Smile at the other people that are in the group. This lets an employer know that you are friendly.

Most group interviews will start out in the waiting room. Do not pull out your cell phone and check messages, email, anything! Put it away. In our interview I watched how people behaved. The ones that smiled at each other, and just sat patiently, or even made friendly small talk, stood out. The woman that pulled out her phone and solely focused on that showed that she wasn't friendly, and didn't seem comfortable in a group setting. How was she going to work in a medical office? Do not be loud or boisterous. This atmosphere is a good place to exhibit your confidence.

One guy came in, he was nicely dressed and I would have considered him, except for one reason. He parked his car right in front of the office and his girlfriend was sitting in it waiting for him. Seriously? He couldn't leave her for an hour for a job interview? I didn't consider him.

You will be taken aside separately and asked a group of questions. The hirer is listening for your answers and watching your composure. Answer honestly, but be unique. The most common question you will be asked (and one which I hate) is, "Tell me your strong points."

Don't say, "Well I really like working with people, I want to help people…" Blah blah blah. Point out something that you know you're good at, and like doing. "I really like educating people, telling them easy things they can do to improve their health." Or, "I like scheduling patients; I found that I'm really good at maximizing the schedule for the doctor, keeping him busy but not overwhelmed." Or, "I really like taking x-rays, and I found out I'm good at it! Patients always seem comfortable." That stuff is good.

My second all-time least favorite question is, "What don't you like to do in the office?" Don't you dare say, "Oh I like doing everything!" Liar. No one likes doing everything. Say something like, "I'm not crazy about calling patients whose bill is overdue, but I found I am very good at collecting money from patients when they are here in the office." Think of answers to those two questions beforehand, and be prepared, but don't sound rehearsed when you answer.

PREVIOUS EMPLOYERS

Of course you are going to be asked about previous employers. Watch what you say.

Let's take the "My boss is a creep" scenario. You may have worked for the world's greatest scumbag, but don't say it. That is your opinion, and your circumstance. Respond by saying, "I wasn't comfortable working for Dr. Scumbag, and I want to become established in an office long-term. I don't think things will change there, so that's why I'm looking for a new job." If you bad-mouth a doctor, the one that is interviewing you will be flagged that you talk about employers openly and easily, and not in a complimentary fashion.

You're in an office that is gossip central. I have been there, and also heard this from others. This is alright to express. Say it tactfully, "The office I am in now doesn't seem to concentrate on work, there are a few people that talk about others and that seems to be their focal point. I don't want to be part of it."

Favoritism. Other employees in the office you're at seem to be the boss's favorites. Been there. Guess what? You will never change them, they will always like the other person better. Don't say it that way, you will look like a whiner. Instead, you can say that you feel you've been overlooked for promotions or raises, and honestly feel it was unfair. You spoke to your boss about it and he/she denied it, but you don't agree. What makes you look good explaining this is that you said you went to your boss and talked to him about it. This shows initiative, and that you aren't sitting there taking it and complaining.

Remember, unless a 19-year-old is interviewing you, and the employer is also 19, they have been in or know of these common, unfortunate situations. What the new employer is wanting to know is how you handled it.

PERSONAL INFORMATION

Another oh boy. This is tricky. Let them ask questions, do not volunteer. Most states will not allow employers to ask if you have children. Most employers want to know this, and will eventually find out. In case you haven't figured this one out, the reason they want to know will be extra time off those with children tend to require.

If you have a child in day care, and the child is sick, you cannot take him to day care. Good chance that you will call in sick to take care of him. However, your mother-in-law stays home all day, junior is sick and that's where he will go. You can come to work with peace of mind. This is a good thing. Let them know this if it comes out in the interview that you do have children. Don't get me wrong, I love children, have a few myself. But, as an employer, I'm looking at potential trouble. There is no magic answer for this, I am just letting you know what they're thinking.

I interviewed a very qualified woman, and she started to tell me about her ill parents and her no-good brother that doesn't help. She is, therefore, responsible for taking care of them. She is getting them into a nursing home, in four months. I needed someone to start immediately. She seemed distracted and a bit overwhelmed with her parents' situation. Believe me, I felt for her. I'm not cold hearted, but there wasn't anything I could do to help her. I was potentially offering her a job, but she wouldn't fulfill her part, by being a focused employee. I actually didn't want to get involved with that intense situation.

What she should have done was to let me know she is in the process of relocating her parents into a nursing home. This shouldn't take time away from work, and all is well. She should not have mentioned the brother (bitterness) and acted as if she had everything under control. I definitely would have been more understanding with that type of attitude.

Do not talk about your dating situation, girlfriends and partying, or all the wonderful things your children have accomplished. One woman went on and on about her two kids. All I could imagine was that she probably had a bumper sticker that says, "My Kid Beat Up Your Honor Student." Seriously, that's how I felt. This shouldn't have come up at all. She should have said, "I do have two children, Susie is 12 and Brian is 14, they are involved in sports. They are old enough to care for themselves when they get home from school." The last sentence of that quote would have made me happy. All I imagined was her having 12 pictures of them in assorted sports uniforms all over her desk, and constantly bugging me for money for fund raisers so they could go to competitions.

Keep your personal information to a minimum. Do not talk negatively about anything, but don't be a bragger.

WORKING INTERVIEW

You've passed the interview and they want you to come back for a working interview. This is what the office wants to accomplish:

- Do you really have the skills you say you do?
- Do you blend with the other employees?

First of all, it is totally appropriate to ask (if they didn't tell you) if you will be paid for this working interview. I've seen it go both ways. You should at least be compensated minimum wage. I have worked half-days without being compensated, because I was very interested in the position and felt it would have been worth my time; I would never work a full eight-hour day without being paid for my time.

Here's a hint, if the office is not going to pay you but wants you to do a full-day working interview, they're cheap. I would not do this interview unless the potential was good, the salary, should they hire you, is higher than what you want, and you would be happy getting up every morning going to work. But I would really weigh everything. *You should be compensated.*

When they tell you about the interview, *pay attention.*

Example: I had one girl I wanted to have return for a working interview. During her interview, while she was dressed nicely and had all the right answers, she was wearing a ton of perfume. I couldn't imagine working next to her in the front office all day, my sinuses would die. So, during the interview I told her, "Your perfume is very pretty, but it is too much to wear in a doctor's office. We have patients with allergies, and we just can't have that." Her response was, "Oh can you smell it?" Duh. The office next door could smell it. I said yes, and repeated, don't wear perfume in the office. Two days later I called her to schedule a working interview. She was excited! I repeated to her the time I wanted her to arrive, which happened to be our early start day. So, I told her to be in the office by 6:30 a.m. since we see our first patients at 7:00 a.m. I repeated this info. She said, "Ok, great, I'm excited, thank you!" The next morning arrived and no potential person. I hesitated calling her because this was a test. If she had an emergency or something unforeseen, she should have called me. At 7:00 a.m the doctor told me, even if she showed up, to send her home. Well 7:20 rolls around and the door opens, and all I smell is perfume. She strolls in smiling huge, and I told her we were expecting her at 6:30. She dropped her jaw saying she thought I said 7:30, and she was feeling good about being early. Here is the lesson: she didn't listen and write down the time I asked her to be there, even after I stressed it was our early start day, twice. And the perfume. An hour after she left the fragrance lingered in the office. She called later asking for a second chance. I informed her we wouldn't do that, and didn't even bring up the perfume again. For record's sake, I did mention the perfume thing to another candidate. When she returned for her working interview, no perfume. She was also on time.

During the interview two things are being observed by the employer:

- How much you know;
- How well you listen.

I had one woman tell me as she was waving her hand at me, "I know how to do this." She may have, but she did not know how *our* office wanted it done. Every office has a specific way they want the phone answered, how they want appointments confirmed, the manner in which they want you to bring a patient back to the operatory, and so forth. When she said this to me, I knew she wouldn't listen when I told her how the doctor wanted things done, or take orders for that matter.

A working interview I was on wanted me to call patients and have them schedule treatment. First thing I did was ask the girl working with me to do one call first, so I could hear the verbiage she used. She did, and I listened. My first call I scheduled a guy for a crown he had been putting off. I got a "high-five" from the dentist.

When I want candidates to call and confirm patients, I make one call first as an example. I also have the verbiage written down so they can read it. So, should you be asked to do something like this, it is appropriate to ask for an example on "how the office/doctor wants it done."

Watch everyone working there. Ask questions, but at the appropriate time, and make sure they are intelligent questions. If you are asked to "shadow" someone, don't stand there like a dummy. I had one girl shadowing an assistant. She literally stood in the operatory with her arms crossed, not saying a word or asking questions. She must have scared the daylights out of the patient that was in the chair! Stand out of the way, but yet move in closer when there is something you want to see. Keep your arms at your side, or hold them behind your back. The doctor will take note of this, and know you are interested and paying attention. Standing against a wall with your arms crossed looking like a zombie doesn't work. She was not asked back.

You must be flexible enough to learn how the doctor/office wants things done. This is NOT the time to make suggestions. I hate it when candidates say, "Well I found it's better if I do it this way, or did you ever try to do it this way?" Suggest this after you are hired. We want to know how/if you follow directions and how you respond when I ask you to do something.

I had a candidate confirming appointments, and told her that we call the patient's cell phone first. Her response was, "Oh, I always call the home phone first." What did I just say? Call the cell phone!

OMG I'M GONNA BE LATE!

Let's re-cap. You have an interview, you googled the office, you drove by so you know exactly where you're going, you printed a resume, you're dressed in a suit and by golly you look good! You're getting ready to walk out the door and your dog is acting funny. You love this dog, you can't just walk out with her being this way, how will you concentrate? You're watching her intently, trying to figure out what to do, when the dog comes over to you and vomits all over your foot. It splashed on your pants, your shoe is disgusting, your foot feels slimy, but puppy is dancing around now and feels better. You have to get completely changed and you will be late! This is what you do:

Clean up the mess as quickly as possible. Throw your pants and shoe in the bathtub, and wash your foot. Put on another pair of pants and shoes, hopefully they match, and go! There is a chance you will still be there on time (you planned to be there early, didn't you?) but if you are still in the car when it is five minutes to your appointment time, call. Do not think you will tell them what happened when you get there and everyone will have a good laugh. No. All they will think is YOU ARE LATE FOR AN INTERVIEW. Call them and tell them as you were leaving you had a minor emergency at home, but it's taken care of and you are SO SORRY and you are just five minutes from the office. When you get there, go to the appropriate person, introduce yourself, apologize sincerely again. If they are very friendly and laid back, they may ask if everything is ok. Don't go into detail, just say your dog got sick on your foot right when you were leaving and you had to change. Don't make a big deal about it. Be sincere.

I had a woman call 20 minutes before her working interview saying her car broke down and she was on the side of the road. I asked if there was anything I could do, call someone for her? She said no, she already did. I asked if she wanted to re-schedule for the afternoon. She said she would call me. Yeah. She changed her mind about the interview, and stood outside to call me so I would think she was on the road. Do you know what she accomplished? Making a fool of herself. I would have had much more respect if she called me and said she changed her mind, she didn't think our office was what she was looking for. If she didn't want to talk to me, she could have called after hours the night before and left me a message. This still would have been better than her lame excuse.

BASIC COMMON SENSE

Making a good impression is really just using common sense. Pay attention to the atmosphere in the office.

I would always go to an interview ten minutes early, so I could just sit in the waiting room. I wanted to "feel" how the office felt. I wanted to listen to the people working, how they spoke to each other and patients. I would imagine me going to that office every morning to work there, would I be comfortable? Would I look forward to going to work?

One very pretty office I went to answered all of my questions before I even had the interview. First thing I noticed, they had a lot, I mean seven or eight, huge posters advertising implants, bleaching, all different types of dental procedures. This was a very pretty office, and all the posters made it look cheap. A few signs are fine, but these were posters.

Second thing, I listened to how the two girls in the front spoke to each other. They were filing charts and just talking, so you could tell their personalities. One seemed friendly; the other wished she were anywhere else. So I'm picturing me working there. I knew I didn't want this job before I met the doctor, and so I declined a working interview.

Unless you are desperate for a job, pay attention to these types of things. If you are looking for something long-term, they are important.

How does the doctor present himself? Does he/she look you in the eye when they shake hands with you? Do they ask you questions and listen to your answers? Do you have their undivided attention during the interview, or are they looking at the computer or talking to others?

One boss I had, said to me about a prospect at the beginning of a working interview, "I know this is the best I will get." Meaning, the prospect will be at their best during a working interview. This goes both ways. If you don't like the way you are treated by the doctor during an interview, remember, this is how you will be treated while you work there. If you don't like the way you are treated, keep looking. You will be the best employee when you are happy going to work. You will value your job and give it your best when it is something you want to keep.

Common sense and maturity are the most important virtues an employer is looking for. I know doctors that would rather train someone who possesses those two qualities, compared to someone that went through school, but weren't ready to face the real business world.

Treat your interview with respect. Shake people's hands and look them in the eye. It's ok if your nervous, often times so is the interviewer. Be professional, after all you're embarking into a field of helping people.

YOU GOT THE JOB

Congratulations you got the job! You got the magic call and you laugh, or cry, with relief. One other thing to keep in mind to assure your success: You're the Newbie. I know you're excited, and you can't wait to be part of the office team. You want to share all your life's journeys with the people there and impress them. Please don't. The best thing that you can do for your career, is to "watch" the people already working there, and hold off on all your stories until you get to know everyone a little bit better. Concentrate on learning your new job and let your coworkers get to know you a little bit at a time.

Let's say you're hired as an additional dental assistant. There are two others in the office; one has a ton of experience, the other only a few years. They both have seniority on you, and the doctor is pleased with them. Watch them, listen to them, and ask them questions. One girl that was hired fresh out of school was convinced she knew everything. Henceforth, she went on so long not respecting the head assistant, she alienated herself from her. This newbie missed out on learning. If she had watched the other two assistants, who clearly made the office run smoothly, the atmosphere would have been better and she would have learned things no school can teach. Instead, she loved to tell stories about herself and didn't feel she had anything else to learn.

Don't be a smarty pants. Watch and learn. Be open minded.

THE END

One last thing. You are advertising you. Live in the moment and focus. Every experience you have adds to your future. Remember this and you'll be great!

Contact Leena at leena.lavage@gmail.com